SURF a

Graphics and Memorabilia

Rod Sumpter

Schiffer Publishing Ltd

4880 Lower Valley Road, Atglen, PA 19310 USA

Other Schiffer Books on Related Subjects
Surf's Up: Collecting the Longboard Era, by Mark Blackburn
Surfing, by Nancy N. Schiffer in cooperation with San Francisco
    Airport Museums
Hula Girls and Surfer Boys, by Mark Blackburn
Hawaiiana: The Best of Hawaiian Design, by Mark Blackburn

Cover and book designed by: Bruce Waters
Type set in Van Dijk/Caslon224 Bk BT

ISBN: 0-7643-2495-0
Printed in China

Published by Schiffer Publishing Ltd.
4880 Lower Valley Road
Atglen, PA 19310
Phone: (610) 593-1777; Fax: (610) 593-2002
E-mail: Info@schifferbooks.com

For the largest selection of fine reference books on this and related subjects, please visit our web
site at www.schifferbooks.com
We are always looking for people to write books on new and related subjects. If you have an idea for a
book please contact us at the above address.

This book may be purchased from the publisher.
Include $3.95 for shipping.
Please try your bookstore first.
You may write for a free catalog.

In Europe, Schiffer books are distributed by
Bushwood Books
6 Marksbury Ave.
Kew Gardens
Surrey TW9 4JF England
Phone: 44 (0) 20 8392-8585; Fax: 44 (0) 20 8392-9876
E-mail: info@bushwoodbooks.co.uk
Website: www.bushwoodbooks.co.uk
Free postage in the U.K., Europe; air mail at cost.

Front cover image: Rod Sumpter surfing at Mollymook, N.S.W. Australia. *Rod Sumpter Collection.*

Acknowledgments

This book would not have been possible without the support, help, and enthusiasm of my wife Valerie, who checked and corrected the manuscript. Thanks to my son John for his enthusiastic surfing and photography, to Sarah, and to baby Ben who lights up our lives. Thanks to Mark and Clare for their photo technology and to Colin and Diana. To Chris and Liz for their research of interesting memorabilia. Special thanks to Jamie and Maria for their collection and the photography of J & L Photography (jandlphoto@comcast.net). Thanks to Keith Maynard Eshelman at the Gallery of Surf Classics (www.surfclassics.com) for his fantastic collection, and to Tim DeLaVega of www.surflit.com.

Also, greatest thanks to Graham Looker, John Baxendale, Susan Darwin, and Andy Pickles. To Simon Skelton, who owns and still rides Rod Sumpter model boards dating from 1965-1966. To Katy Goodwin, for the abstract painting of Rod Sumpter (for commissions, call +44 (0)1271 890706), and to Eddie Hoskin for the nose riding mural of the author on a good day.

Any omissions for copy or credit are unintentional and credit will be given in future editions. For details regarding Rod Sumpter surf photo and art work, e-mail rodsumpter@rodsumpter.fsnet.co.uk.

Introduction

During the mid to late 1950s, I rode the waves at South and North Avalon beach in Australia, joining a select group of breakaway surfboard riders who became young wave hunters and starred in the new entertainment of the day—the surf movie. I had learned to body surf in 1954 and received my first surfoplane for Christmas of 1955. In 1955 and 1956, I started retrieving the 16-foot hollow plywood boards from many a wipe-out by the big guys who were all members of the Avalon Surf Life Saving Club, and I'd ride the board on shore waves before the surfer swam in to claim it (no leashes in those days). It was an era of waves and surfing and new equipment.

When the 10-foot solid balsa Malibu board was introduced to Australia by the Duke Kahanamoko Hawaiian and Californian surf team at a 1956 exhibition, it amazed us all and changed my life. On that day, the crowd on the beach stood and watched in awe as time and time again the Malibu board performed unimaginable feats. This new type of board brought cornering, speed trimming through white water, and turning back and forth. Within two years it brought about two culture-changing phenomena: the nose rides of hanging ten and the birth of surf movie entertainment. This culture of surf, sport, beach beat, and Friday night surf stomps echoed the thrilling experiences we had riding big, small, and hollow waves. The technique of shaping better board designs went hand in hand with photography, filmmaking, and the surfing lifestyle.

"You should have been here yesterday," are the words I spoke in *The Endless Summer* film of 1964. As that sentiment conveys, there is no greater pleasure than reliving the past with a good book of surfing memorabilia to help us remember our most enjoyable rides, our wipe-outs, and our big surfing moments. As a hoarder and collector, I liked being the first to attend a surf movie and asking for the poster—this was my passion as much as dawn surfing patrols. Hoarding, always hoarding. I knew that one day I would enjoy using the material I collected to reminisce about a certain date or event or who did what and where—that it would become part of surfing history. And of course, part of the fun of collecting was meeting the great people of the era.

I have compiled this book with as much accuracy as possible and I've included a general auction valuation of the items. Great friends and fantastic collectors have joined with me in contributing wonderful pieces of surf memorabilia. I hope you feel as exhilarated as I do by the book. It is not only a paper trail of early surfing life, it includes some high points of my youth. Enjoy this window into the past that honors a magical era of surfing.

—Rod Sumpter

Contents

Chapter 1

Movie Posters, Handbills, and Lobby Cards

Surfing Hollow Days, 1962. © Bruce Brown.
Keith Eshelman Collection. $175.

Surfing Hollow Days, 1962. © Bruce Brown.
Rod Sumpter Collection. $175.

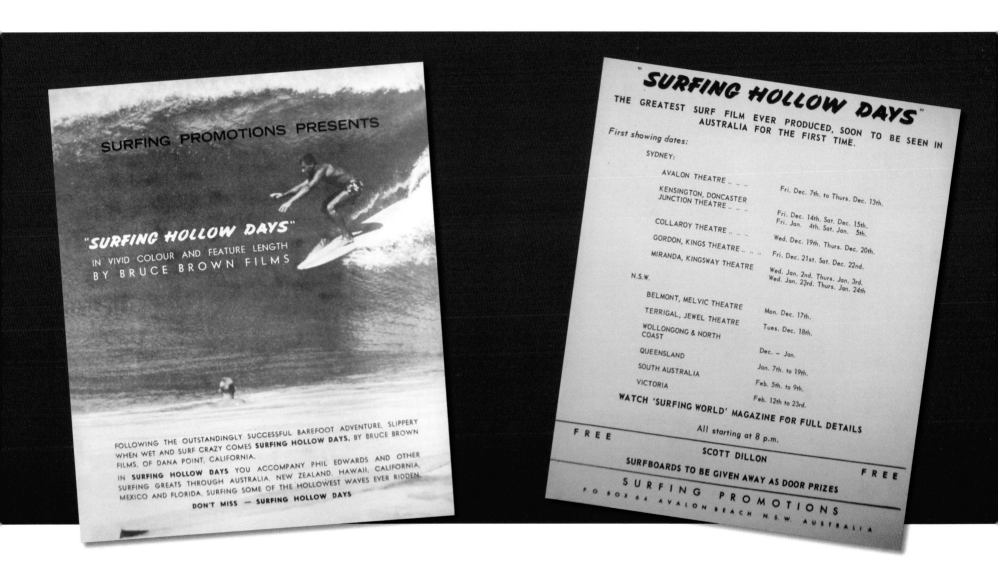

Surfing Hollow Days, handbill, Australia, 1963.
Rod Sumpter Collection. $25.

Surfing Hollow Days, handbill, Australia, 1963.
Rod Sumpter Collection. $25.

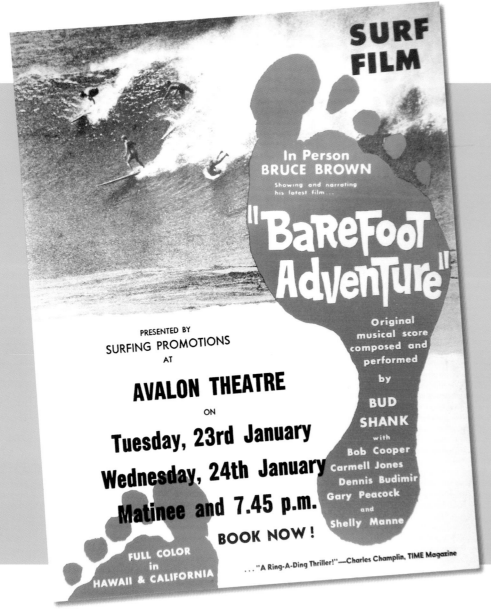

Barefoot Adventure, 1962. © Bruce Brown.
Rod Sumpter Collection. $200.

Barefoot Adventure and *Surfing Hollow Days*,
handbill, 1961-62. *Rod Sumpter Collection. $75.*

NEW! DIFFERENT!

AUSTRALIA'S FIRST FULL LENGTH DOUBLE FEATURE SURF FILM

• DENNIS MILNE'S
SURF STOMP

• DENNIS ELTON'S
FOLLOW THE SURF!

IN FULL COLOUR WITH SOUND TRACK

COLLAROY SURF CLUB — SATURDAY 9TH MARCH

AVOLON SURF CLUB — SATURDAY 16TH MARCH

AT 8 P.M.

Surf Stomp and *Follow the Surf*, 1961. © Dennis Milnes,
© Dennis Elton. *Rod Sumpter Collection*. $500.

The Surf Movie, 1973. © MacGillivray and
Freeman. *Keith Eshelman Collection*. $100.

The Last Wave, 1965. © Grant Rohloff.
Keith Eshelman Collection. $150.

For Surfers Only, 1964. © Grant Rohloff.
Keith Eshelman Collection. $150.

North Swell, 1963. © Grant Rohloff.
Keith Eshelman Collection. $175.

The Living Curl, 1965. © Jamie Budge.
Keith Eshelman Collection. $125.

Follow That Surf, 1963. © Bill Singer.
Keith Eshelman Collection. $125.

Hot Dog on a Stick, 1962. © Bill Stromberg.
Keith Eshelman Collection. $150.

Hot Dog on a Stick, 1962. © Bill Stromberg.
Keith Eshelman Collection. $250.

Have Board Will Travel, 1963. © Don Brown.
Keith Eshelman Collection. $175.

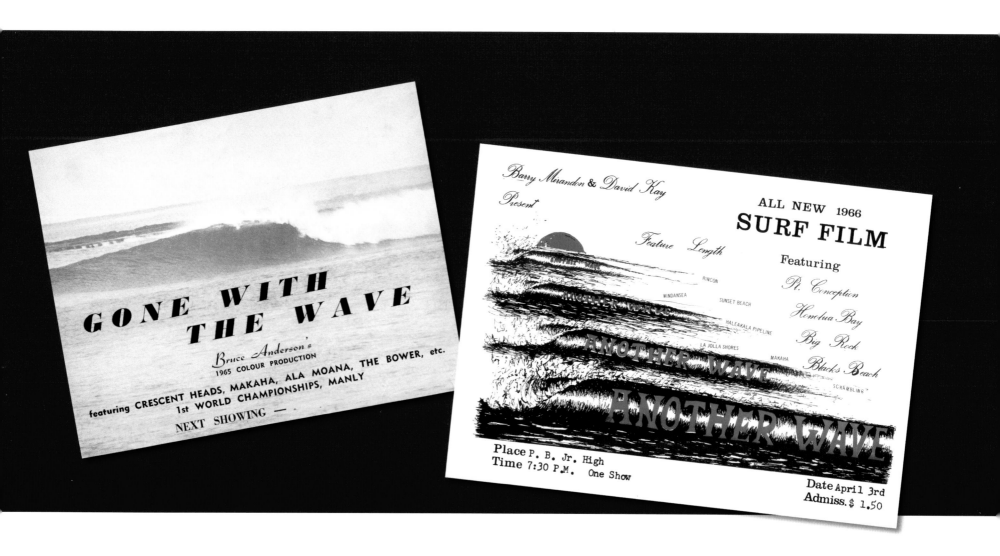

Gone With the Wave, 1964. © Bruce Anderson.
Keith Eshelman Collection. $125.

Another Wave, 1966. © Barry Mirandon.
Keith Eshelman Collection. $125.

Sacrifice for Surf, 1960. © Bob Bagley.
Keith Eshelman Collection. $175.

Pipeline, 1963. © Walt Phillips.
Keith Eshelman Collection. $125.

Psyche Out, 1962. © Walt Phillips.
Keith Eshelman Collection. $150.

Cavalcade of Surf, 1964. © Bud Browne.
Keith Eshelman Collection. $150.

Spinning Boards, 1961. © Bud Browne.
Keith Eshelman Collection. $150.

Spinning Boards and *Cavalcade of Surf*, 1962. © Bud Browne
and Dale Davis. *Keith Eshelman Collection.* $175.

Cavalcade of Surf, 1962. © Bud Browne; *Spinning Boards*.
© Bud Browne. *Rod Sumpter Collection*. $150.

The Young Wave Hunters, 1962. © Bob Evans.
Rod Sumpter Collection. $250.

Big Wednesday, 1978. *Keith Eshelman Collection.* $30-50.

Surf Down Under, 1958. © Bud Browne.
Keith Eshelman Collection. $175.

The Fantastic Plastic Machine, lobby card, 1969.
Keith Eshelman Collection. $40.

Pacific Vibrations, lobby card, 1970.
Keith Eshelman Collection. $40.

The Endless Summer, lobby card, 1964.
Keith Eshelman Collection. $200.

The Endless Summer, handbill, 1964.
Rod Sumpter Collection. $40.

Once Upon A Wave, 1963. © Walt Phillips.
Rod Sumpter Collection. $150.

Search For Surf, 1957. © Greg Noll.
Keith Eshelman Collection. $200.

Fiberglass Jungle, 1962. © Dale Davis.
Keith Eshelman Collection. $150.

Surfing The Southern Cross, 1963. © Bob Evans.
Rod Sumpter Collection. $450.

Surf Mania, 1961. © Walt Phillips.
Rod Sumpter Collection. $175.

Outside The Third Dimension, 1964. © Jim Freeman.
Keith Eshelman Collection. $175.

The Performers, 1965. © Greg MacGillivray.
Keith Eshelman Collection. $150.

Free and Easy, 1967. © MacGillivray and Freeman.
Keith Eshelman Collection. $150.

Long Live The Waves, 1963. © John Williams.
Rod Sumpter Collection. $300.

Out Of Control, 1965. © Grant Rohloff.
Rod Sumpter Collection. $75.

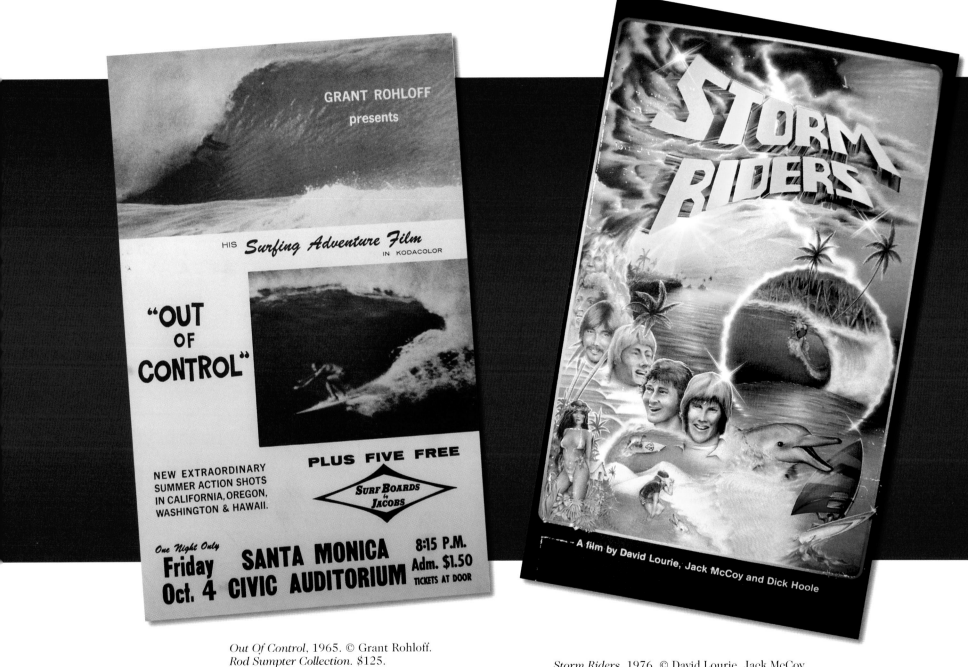

Out Of Control, 1965. © Grant Rohloff.
Rod Sumpter Collection. $125.

Storm Riders, 1976. © David Lourie, Jack McCoy,
Dick Hoole. *Graham Looker Collection.* $40.

*A Sea for Yourself, 1971. Rod
Sumpter Collection. $125.*

*Gun Ho, 1967. © Bud Brown.
Rod Sumpter Collection. $350.*

Water-Logged, 1963. © Bruce Brown.
Rod Sumpter Collection. $200.

Water-Logged, handbill, 1964.
Rod Sumpter Collection. $40.

Viva Las Olas, 1966. © John Williams.
Rod Sumpter Collection. $75.

A Life In The Sun, 1966. © Paul Witzig.
Rod Sumpter Collection. $175.

"A Life in the Sun" Was shown to-night by Dave + Rodney Sumpter at their own expense..... If you liked the film please show your gratitude with a donation.

ROD SUMPTER presents

'COME SURF WITH ME'

90 minute COLOUR FILM with sound
★ Travelling and Surfing ★
in
CORNWALL · IRELAND · FRANCE
★SEVERN BORE TIDAL WAVE
BRITAIN'S FIRST SURFING FILM

St. Michael's Hall

ST. MICHAEL'S ROAD,
Newquay
MAY 28th, June 4th and 11th
Every Tuesday and Thursday from
July 2nd — August 22nd. at 8.30 p.m.
ADULTS 5/- CHILDREN 2/6
IDEAL FAMILY ENTERTAINMENT

A Life In The Sun, lobby card, 1966. © Rod Sumpter.
Rod Sumpter Collection. $175.

Come Surf With Me, 1965. © Rod Sumpter.
Rod Sumpter Collection. $450.

With Surfing In Mind, 1967. © Rod Sumpter.
Rod Sumpter Collection. $75.

Standing Room Only, 1968. © J. Perkinson.
Rod Sumpter Collection. $50.

Freeform, 1970. © Rod Sumpter. *Rod Sumpter Collection.* $75.

Freeform, Germany. © Rod Sumpter. *Rod Sumpter Collection.* $250.

Freeform II, handbill, 1971. *Rod Sumpter Collection.* $25.

Tales From The Tube, 1975. © Bob Cording,
J. Humphries. *Rod Sumpter Collection*. $50.

The Hot Generation, Europe, 1969. © Paul Witzig.
Rod Sumpter Collection. $50.

Salt Water Wine, French, 1970. © Alan Rich.
Rod Sumpter Collection. $75.

Salt Water Wine, handbill, 1972.
Rod Sumpter Collection. $25.

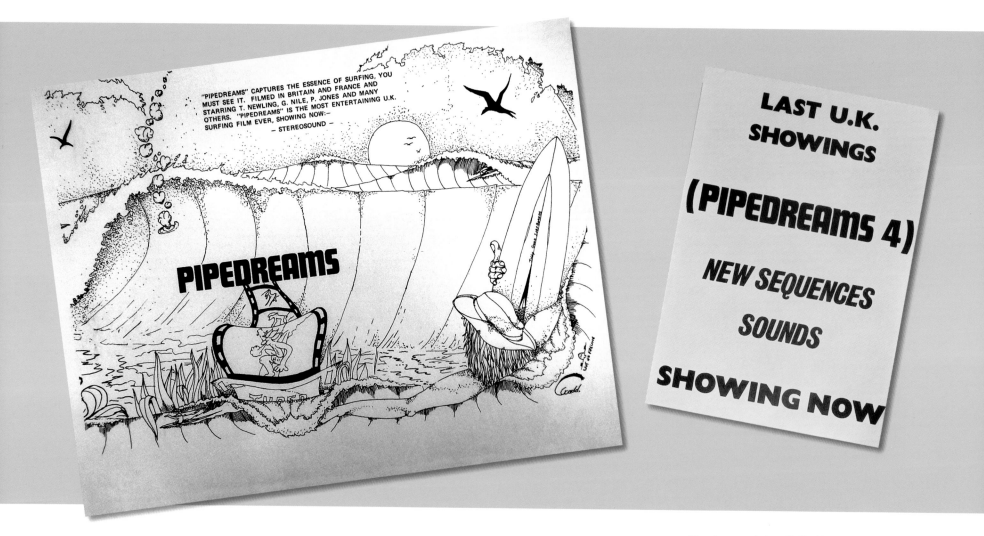

Pipedreams, 1975. © Rod Sumpter.
Rod Sumpter Collection. $50.

Pipedreams 4, handbill, 1974.
Rod Sumpter Collection. $30.

In Natural Flow, 1973. © Steve Core.
Rod Sumpter Collection. $50.

On Any Morning, 1974. © David Sumpter.
Rod Sumpter Collection. $75.

Going Surfing, 1976. © Bud Brown. *Rod Sumpter Collection.* $50.

Oceans handbill, 1971. *Rod Sumpter Collection.* $30.

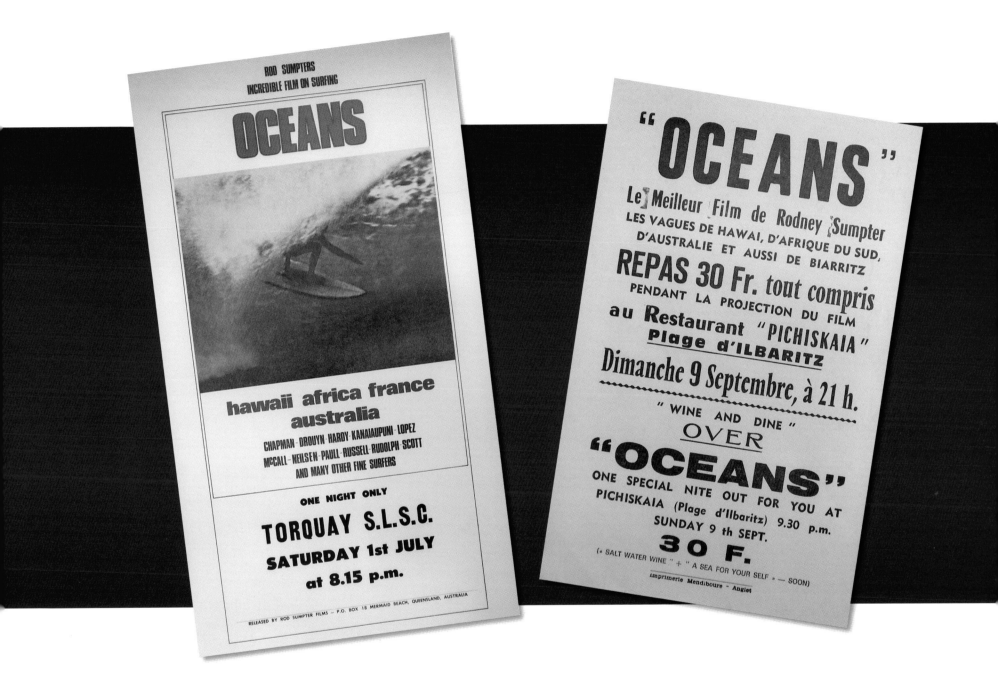

Oceans mk 1, 1971. © Rod Sumpter.
Rod Sumpter Collection. $150.

Oceans handbill, 1972. *Rod Sumpter Collection.* $25.

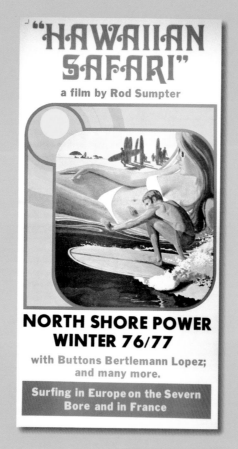

Hawaiian Safari, Japan, 1977.
Rod Sumpter Collection. $25.

Hawaiian Safari mk 2, 1977. © Rod Sumpter.
Rod Sumpter Collection. $175.

The Innermost Limits of Pure Fun, reviews.
Graham Looker Collection. $75.

Pax film festival poster, France,
1973. *Rod Sumpter Collection.* $50.

Films de Surf handbill, 1976.
Rod Sumpter Collection. $25.

"Surfing Films" handbill, 1971.
Graham Looker Collection. $40.

Surf Fever ticket stub. Keith Eshelman Collection. $30-50.

The Endless Summer ticket stub. Keith Eshelman Collection. $30-50.

Have Board Will Travel ticket stub. Keith Eshelman Collection. $30-50.

Gun Ho ticket stub. *Keith Eshelman Collection.* $30-50.

Outside the Third Dimension ticket stub. *Keith Eshelman Collection.* $30-50.

A Cool Wave of Color ticket stub. *Keith Eshelman Collection.* $30-50.

The Angry Sea ticket stub. *Keith Eshelman Collection.* $30-50.

The Performers ticket stub. *Keith Eshelman Collection.* $30-50.

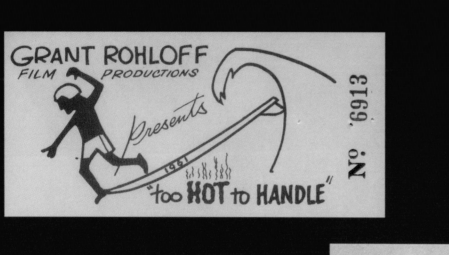

GRANT ROHLOFF
FILM PRODUCTIONS

Presents

1961

"too HOT to HANDLE"

Nº 6913

JOHN SEVERSON
PRESENTS
GOING
MY
WAVE

1962
COLOR
SURF
MOVIE

ADMIT 1

Adm. $1.23; Tx. .02 Tot.$1.25

Nº 17526

JOHN SEVERSON FILMS
Present
SURF CLASSICS
1964 COLOR
SURF MOVIE

Admit 1 — Adm. $1.46
Tax .... .05
Total $1.51

Nº   521

BILL STROMBERG PRESENTS—

HOT DOG
ON A
STICK FEATURING, DYNOMOTION
COLOR STEREO-SOUND

Nº   1423

CALIFORNIA   MEXICO   THE SECRET SPOT

Too Hot to Handle ticket stub. *Keith Eshelman Collection.* $30-50.

Surf Classics ticket stub. *Keith Eshelman Collection.* $30-50.

Going My Wave ticket stub. *Keith Eshelman Collection.* $30-50.

Hot Dog on a Stick ticket stub. *Keith Eshelman Collection.* $30-50.

Viva Las Olas ticket stub. *Keith Eshelman Collection.* $30-50.

Greg Noll ticket stub. *Keith Eshelman Collection.* $30-50.

Surfstomp dance ticket, 1965. *Rod Sumpter Collection.* $30.

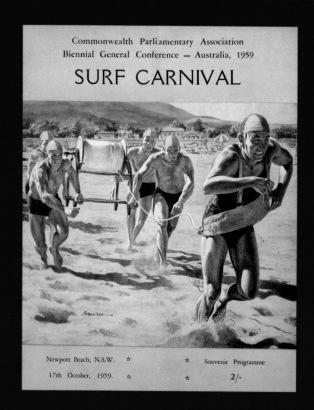

Surf Carnival program, 1959. *Rod Sumpter Collection.* $60.

Surf Life Saving Association of Great Britain, Ladies' Championships program, 1968. *Graham Looker Collection.* $50.

Jersey program, Great Britain National and International Surfboard Championships, 1968. *Rod Sumpter Collection.* $30.

World Contest program, 1970. *Graham Looker Collection.* $150.

Great Britain Championships program, 1969. *Rod Sumpter Collection.* $40.

Great Britain Championships program, 1971. *Graham Looker Collection.* $40.

British Championships program, 1969. *Rod Sumpter Collection.* $30.

European/French Championships, 1975. *Rod Sumpter Collection.* $30.

Entry form, Interstate Surf Meet, entry form, 1963. *Rod Sumpter Collection.* $35.

GREAT BRITAIN SURFBOARD CHAMPIONSHIPS
ST. OUEN'S BAY, JERSEY
CHANNEL ISLANDS .

Sponsored by:—
"PLAYERS GOLD LEAF"

ENTRY BLANK

Age................ Date of Birth................

Name..

Address..

Surf Club................ Entry Fee 5/- per event.

LIST OF EVENTS

1. Great Britain National Surfriding Championship Senior (Over 18 years). ☐
2. Great Britain National Surfriding Championship—Junior (Under 18 years on 31st January, 1966). ☐
3. Great Britain National Surfriding Championship—Ladies. ☐
4. Great Britain International Surfriding Championship. Open to International Surfers and The 1966 Great Britain National Champion. ☐
5. Great Britain Surfboard Paddling Championship—Open to National and International Competitors. ☐

(Events 1, 2, 3, restricted to Competitors born in Great Britain.)

NOTE:—PLACE X IN BOX FOR EVENT YOU ARE ENTERING.

Events will be held on AUGUST 13th and 14th all contestants must report at St. Ouen's Beach before 1 p.m. on each day. Event scheduling will be determined by surf conditions at the time. Entry blanks and fees must be returned to organising chairman, D. S. GRIMSHAW, REDRUTH, LANGLEY AVENUE, ST. SAVIOUR, JERSEY, on or before MONDAY, AUGUST 1st. This deadline is final for all entries.

In consideration of the acceptance by The Great Britain Surfing Championships Committee of my entry into the above checked events the undersigned hereby releases the sponsors, their officers and members, and the officials of said events from any liability arising from bodily injury or property damage which may be sustained by the undersigned as a result of entry into said events or demonstrations.

Signature of Contestant................

Date signed................
Entry fee enclosed:—
Cash   Cheque   Money Order

Phone and Address................

THIS ENTRY WILL NOT BE ACCEPTED WITHOUT YOUR SIGNATURE
OR WITHOUT THE ENTRY FEE

Entry blanks may be obtained at the following places:

M. Carr, Esq.,
"Modern Man",
15E Causeway Head,
Penzance,
Cornwall.

Joel de Rosnay,
1 Rue Charles Lamoureaux,
Paris 16,
France.

Organising Chairman,
G.B. Surfing Championships
D. S. Grimshaw, Esq.,
"Redruth" Langley Avenue,
St. Saviour,
Jersey, C.I.

AUSTRALIAN SURFRIDERS' ASSOCIATION
VICTORIAN BRANCH
P.O. BOX NO. 35 BRIGHTON EAST, VICTORIA, AUSTRALIA
PHONE: XB 3524 [After 5 p.m.]

OPEN
BELLS BEACH ANNUAL BOARDRIDING RALLY
AND
VICTORIAN CHAMPIONSHIPS

To qualify for both events, competitors must be financial members of the Victorian Branch of the Australian Surfriders' Association or their recognised equivalent State Associations.

Entries close by mail 12 p.m. 23rd March, 1964 for ALL competitors.

Details of heats at Lot 204, Camping area, Torquay, on Good Friday.

* **Note:— There will be no entry fee but Membership cards must be produced.**

FOR VICTORIANS ONLY —

If you wish to compete in the "World Championships" in Sydney on May 15th and 16th. *Please Mark in Appropriate Square on Entry Form Below.*

Victoria has been allotted the following entries. 18 Senior; 14 Junior; 5 Women Competitors.

Only Members who compete over Easter in the Bells Rally will be eligible to compete in Sydney in the World Championships.

Therefore the filling of these allotments will be decided at the Bells Beach Annual Board Rally over Easter.

Ampol will fully sponsor the Victorian Senior, Junior and Women's champion to Sydney for these championships, and present Ampol trophies for 1st, 2nd and 3rd in each of these events.

ENTRY FORM FOR ALL COMPETITORS

Name................
[USE BLOCK LETTERS]

Address................

Age................
(age at 17th May, 1964)   Date of Birth................

Association................

Membership No.................

Normal Surfing Beach................

tick which
is
Applicable

Senior Mens ☐
Junior Mens ☐
Womens ☐

Juniors must be under 18 on the 17th May, 1964.

If you wish to compete in the "World Championships" in Sydney on May 15th and 16th.
Please tick ☐

Post this entry form to Box 35, Brighton East, Victoria, by March 23rd.

Entry form, Great Britain Surfboard Championships, 1966. *Rod Sumpter Collection.* $25.

Entry form, Australian Surfriders' Association, 1964. *Rod Sumpter Collection.* $25.

Gorden and Smith, 1962. *Rod Sumpter Collection. $25.*

Keyo Surfboards, 1963. *Rod Sumpter Collection. $30.*

Kanvas by Katin, 1964. *Keith Eshelman Collection. $75.*

Birdwell Beach Britches, 1964. *Keith Eshelman Collection.* $75.

Surfboards by Jacobs, 1964. *Keith Eshelman Collection.* $125.

Greg Noll Surfboards, 1963. *Keith Eshelman Collection.* $150.

Velzyland, 1964. *Rod Sumpter Collection.* $30.

Surf Shop, 1962. *Rod Sumpter Collection.* $80.

Holland Surfing Association, 1968.
Rod Sumpter Collection. $30.

Australian Surfer Magazine, 1962.
Rod Sumpter Collection. $75.

Barefoot Adventure, 1961-62.
Rod Sumpter Collection. $50.

Hobie Surfboards, 1964. *Rod
Sumpter Collection.* $25.

1820 Pacific Coast Hwy. Hermosa Bch. FR. 2-1248

Ampol, 1964. *Rod Sumpter Collection.* $40.

Bing Surfboards, 1964. *Rod Sumpter Collection.* $25.

Surfing Promotions, 1966. *Rod Sumpter Collection.* $25.

Atlas, New Zealand, 1964. *Rod Sumpter Collection. $40.*

North East West Surf Club, 1967. *John Baxendale Collection.*

The remainder of the decals in this chapter date from the 1980s to 2000 and are valued from $5-15 each. All are from the collection of the author.

DISCOVERY SOUTH DEVON
SURF SCHOOL ®
☎ 07813 639 622
www.discoverysurf.com

TUNNEL VISION
SURF SHOP

Robert August
PRECISION SURFBOARDS

EMOCEANL
www.livetosurf.co.uk

surfinglife
PLYMOUTH

60

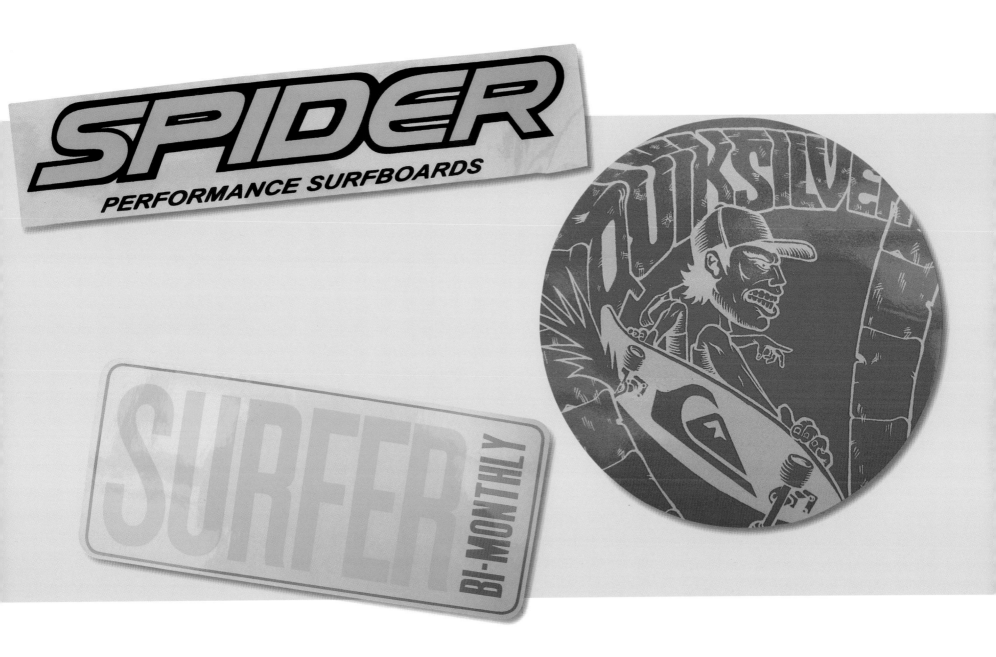

SPIDER
PERFORMANCE SURFBOARDS

SURFER BI-MONTHLY

QUIKSILVER

DESIGN

a Design original
by Rodney Sumpter

QUISILVER

BOARDRIDERS CLUB

surf
ZUMA JAY
www.zumajay.co.uk

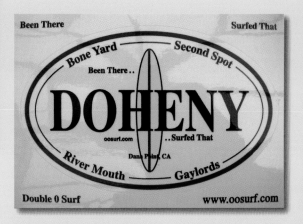

SURF
TEL:
0839·360·PLUS

SCOTLAND
362

WALES
361

EAST COAST
363

SOUTH WEST
360

SOUTH COAST
364

DAILY SURF CONDITIONS
WEEKEND SURF FORECAST

CALL

SURFCALL
Tel:
SURF REPORT
09068
360 360
SURF & BEACH CONDITIONS
DAILY 24 hours
60pp min

MALIBU
BOARDS
CANOES AND

SURREY
SKATEBOARDS
surreyskateboards.com   27 Chertsey Road Woking Surrey
SINCE 1977

KANGAROO POO · SURF WAX · OLD SCHOOL SATIN

BLACK ROCK SURF CO

surfers against sewage
www.sas.org.uk

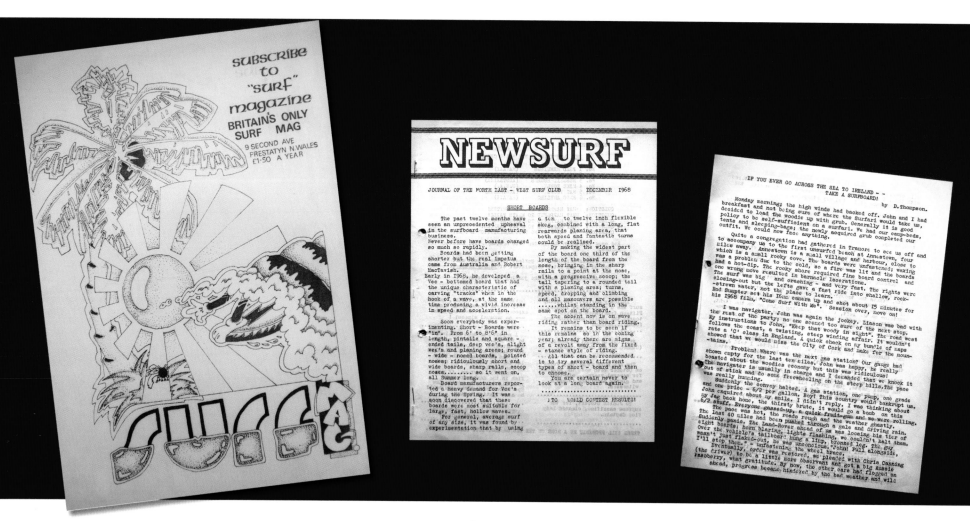

Surf magazine, 1972. *Rod Sumpter Collection. $30.*

Newsurf magazine, 1968. *John Baxendale Collection. $40.*

Newsurf article by D. Thompson, 1968. "If you ever go across the sea to Ireland – take a surfboard!" *John Baxendale Collection. $50.*

Surf Insight, 1972. *Graham Looker Collection*. $50.

Surf Insight, 1973. *Rod Sumpter Collection*. $50.

Surfer magazine cover, 1961. *Graham Looker Collection*. $75.

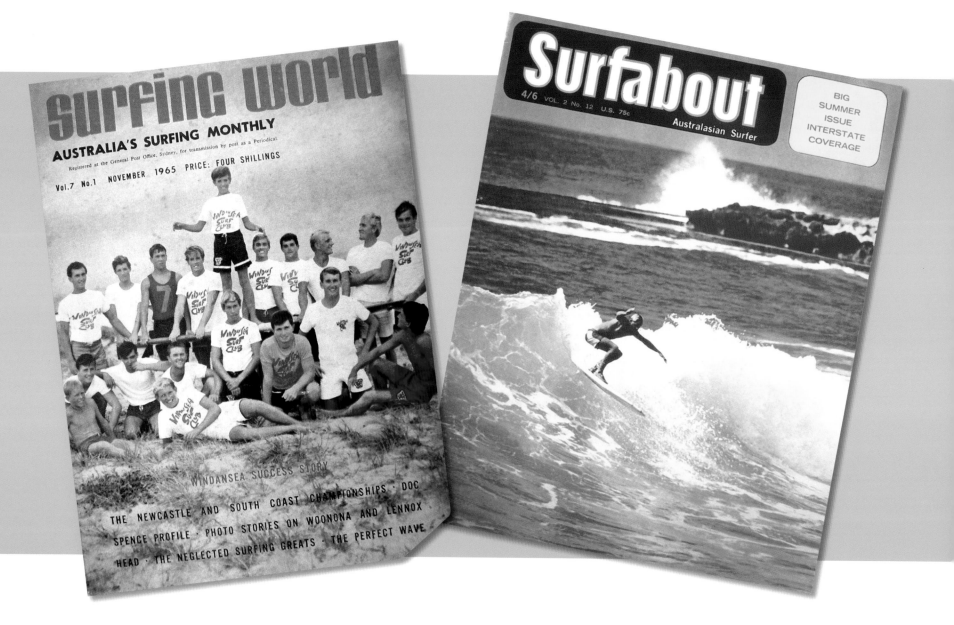

Surfing World, 1965. Graham Looker Collection. $350.

Surfabout magazine, 1962. Rod Sumpter Collection. $150.

Surfabout magazine, 1963.
Rod Sumpter Collection. $50.

American Cinematographer, 1978.
Rod Sumpter Collection. $50.

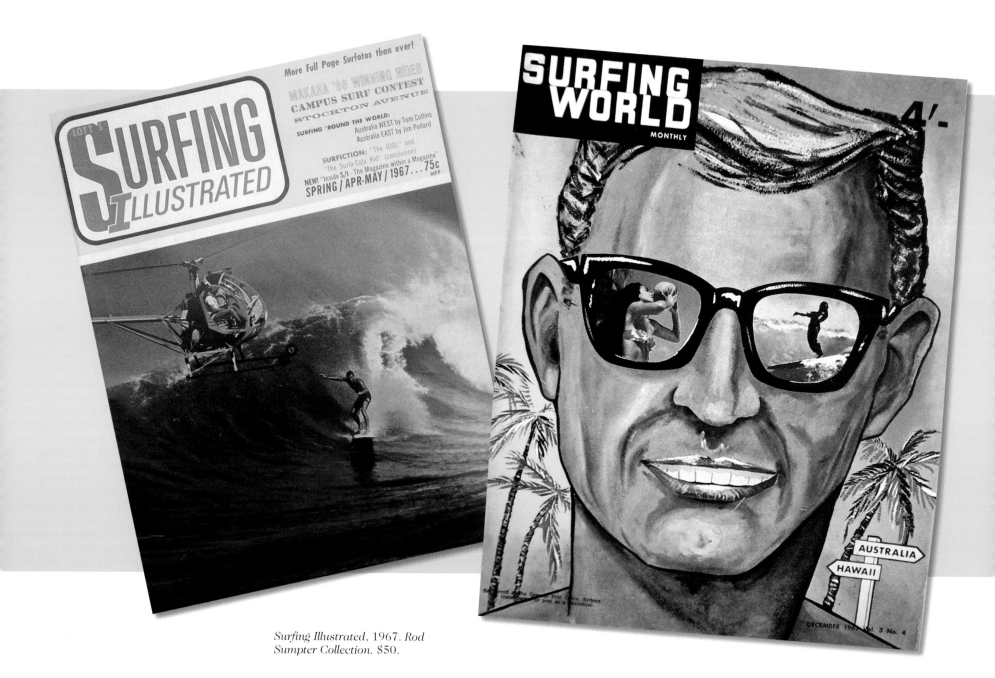

More Full Page Surfotos than ever!

MAKAHA '66 WINNING RIDES
CAMPUS SURF CONTEST
STOCKTON AVENUE

SURFING 'ROUND THE WORLD:
Australia WEST by Tom Collins
Australia EAST by Jim Pollard

SURFICTION: "The IDOL" and
"The Surfa-Cola Kid" (conclusion)

NEW! "Inside S/I - The Magazine within a Magazine"
SPRING / APR-MAY / 1967 . . . 75c

Surfing Illustrated, 1967. Rod
Sumpter Collection. $50.

Surfing World, 1963. Rod Sumpter Collection. $40.

THE SURFING WORLD MONTHLY

PRICE 3'6

OUR OWN "MIDGET" FARRELLY
1963 WORLD CHAMPION BOARD RIDER

FEBRUARY 196
Vol. 1.

Registered at the General Post Office
for transmission by post as a Periodical

THE SURFING WORLD MONTHLY

3'6

THE AUSTRALIAN SURFING MAGAZINE

MARCH 1963
Vol. 2. No. 1.

Registered at the General Post Office, Sydney
for transmission by post as a Periodical

*Surfing World, 1963. Rod Sumpter
Collection. $60.*

*Surfing World, 1963. Rod Sumpter
Collection. $250.*

*British Surfer, 1967. Rod
Sumpter Collection. $80.*

*British Surfer, 1967. Rod
Sumpter Collection. $70.*

*British Surfer, 1966. Rod
Sumpter Collection. $50.*

*British Surfer, 1967. Rod
Sumpter Collection. $60.*

British Surfer, 1968. *Rod Sumpter Collection*. $50.

Shark magazine, 1963. *Rod Sumpter Collection*. $40.

Board Rider, 1961. Rod
Sumpter Collection. $190.

Breezy Stories magazine with surfing
cover, Sept. 1936. No surfing content.
Tim DeLaVega Collection. $100.

New Adventure Comics. Craig Flessel, "Surfing boy cover #18," Aug. 1937. No surfing content. *Tim DeLaVega Collection.* $750.00.

Paradise magazine, 1960. *Rod Sumpter Collection.* $250.

Travel magazine, artist unknown, June 1939. Wonderful image with great Matson ad of wahine laying on surfboard on the back leaf. *Tim DeLaVega Collection.* $150.00.

Surf Guide, 1970. Rod Sumpter Collection. $40.

Surf, 1975. Rod Sumpter Collection. $30.

The Mid-Pacific Magazine, Sept. 1912. A.R. Gurrey photo with another inside, no surfing text. This magazine was primarily devoted to Pan-Pacific culture and policy, but also published many articles about surf riding, especially during its first ten years. *Tim DeLaVega Collection. $50.*

Surf Chat, 1973. *Rod Sumpter Collection.* $25.

Reef Magazine, 1960. *Jamie & Maria Clark Collection.*
$1200-2000 for three issue set.

Surf Jet newsletter, 1969. *Rod Sumpter Collection.* $40.

Five Summer Stories, U.K. program,
1975. *Rod Sumpter Collection.* $50.

Chapter 6

Photographs

The Surf-Rider, c. 1908+. Postcard of unknown wahine. *Tim DeLaVega Collection.* $250.

Waikiki Inn, 1917. Original silver print of Waikiki Inn surfboard and tourist. *Tim DeLaVega Collection.* $250.00.

Vera, 1939, silver print. *Tim DeLaVega Collection.* $50.00.

Des and Ken Thompson, Rhosneigr, Anglesey Island, 1966. *John Baxendale Collection*. $50.

First Malibu's on island, Rhosneigr, Anglesey Island, 1966. *John Baxendale Collection*. $40.

John Baxendale at Sumpters Point, Cable Bay, Anglesey, 1966. *John Baxendale Collection*. $180.

West coast of Ireland, first Irish surfer Kevin Cavey on left, 1966. *John Baxendale Collection.* $30.

Australian Johnny Macaroy at County Kerry, 1966. *John Baxendale Collection.* $75.

Newquay Woody, 1965. Photo: Graham Looker. *Graham Looker Collection.* $275.

Newquay Woody in snow, 1965. Photo: Graham Looker. *Graham Looker Collection.* $175.

Fistral Beach, surfing in snow, 1965. Photo: Graham Looker. *Graham Looker Collection.* $75.

Toots Minvielle, circa 1927. Silver print that shows the famous beach boy and the entrance to the Outrigger Canoe Club. *Tim DeLaVega Collection.* $500.

J.Baxendale, U.K.'s pioneer board builder, 1963. *John Baxendale Collection.*$30.

Rod Sumpter, St Quens Jersey, Channel Islands, 1965. *Rod Sumpter Collection.* $80.

Mural of Rod Sumpter, Molymook Beach, 1962. *Rod Sumpter Collection.* $250.

Chapter 7

Advertising Memorabilia

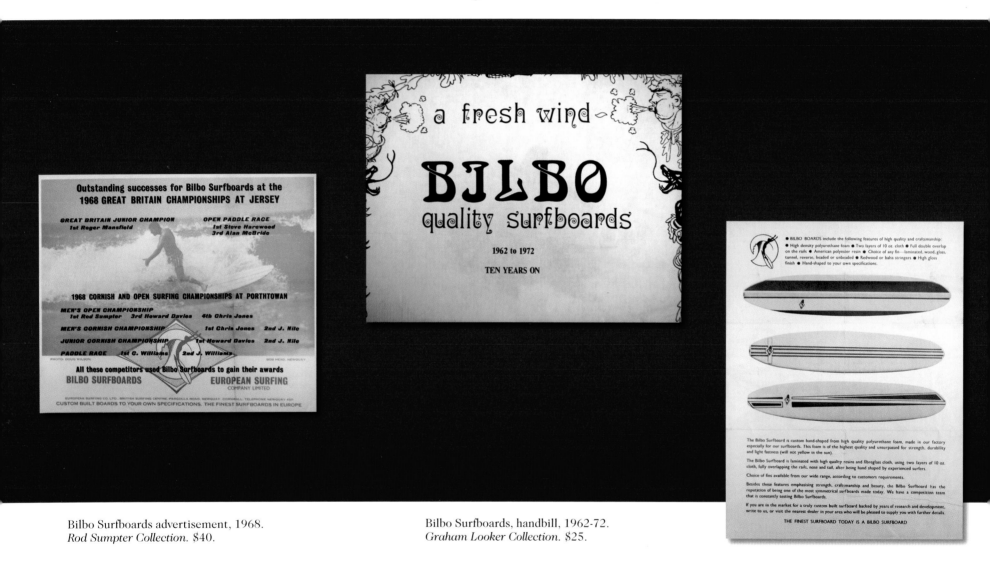

Bilbo Surfboards advertisement, 1968.
Rod Sumpter Collection. $40.

Bilbo Surfboards, handbill, 1962-72.
Graham Looker Collection. $25.

Bilbo ad, 1965. *Rod Sumpter Collection.* $25.

Bilbo list, 1965. *Rod Sumpter Collection.* $30.

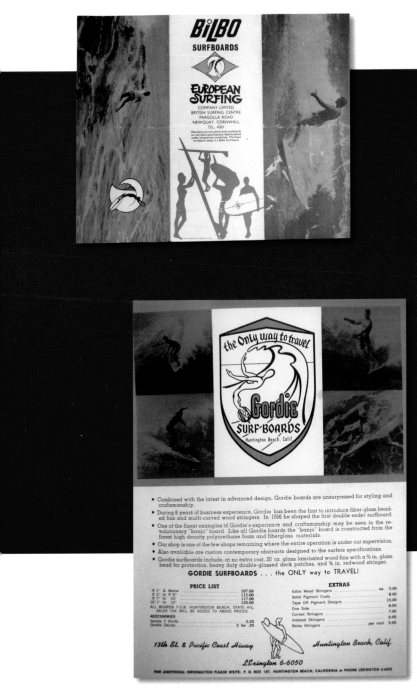

Dewey Weber price list, 1964.
Rod Sumpter Collection. $50.

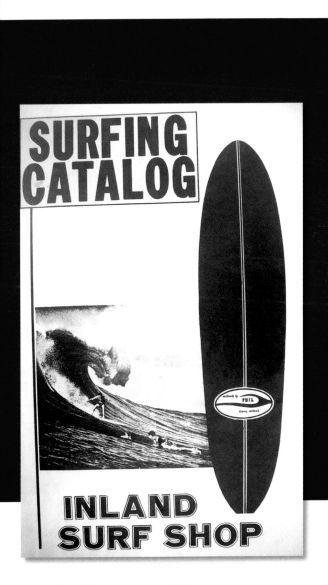

Inland Surf Shop catalogue, 1965.
Rod Sumpter Collection. $30.

Gordie price list, 1964. *Rod Sumpter Collection.* $35.

Maui Surf Shop, handbill, 1969. *Rod Sumpter Collection.* $25.

Big-Gun Surfers, handbill, 1966. *Rod Sumpter Collection.* $25.

Atlas Woods, handbill, 1963. *Rod Sumpter Collection.* $30.

Surfboard Repairs, handbill, 1968.
Rod Sumpter Collection. $25.

SURFBOARD REPAIRS...
59 THE BOULEVARDE CARINGBAH
NiGeL DWYER — 524-2700

SURFERS STORE
THE DIGEY
ST. IVES, CORNWALL
TELEPHONE ST. IVES 5007

so money's
no object...
why object
to paying
less?

New Dolphin wet suits are for discriminators

They know that you don't always have to pay the most to get the best. Now and then along comes someone who gives you the quality you're looking for at a price too good to believe.

Dolphin wet suits come in two ranges —Standard and Super, and large stocks are held of both. As an example of Dolphin value, a two-piece stitched and nylon-lined wet suit in the Standard range is priced at £17.40

In the Super range — made from French NEPEX material, finished to the highest standards and equal in quality to the very best suits available anywhere—a two-piece suit costs £20.95

All Dolphin wet suits are available direct to the customer and we have a very efficient mail order service — with no extra charge for postage and packing.

Write for illustrated brochure/price list.

DOLPHIN Wet Suits Ltd. (856) 69 HATFIELD ROAD, ST. ALBANS, HERTS. Phone St. Albans 50662

LEADERS IN THE BATTLE FOR A LOWER COST WET SUIT

St. Ives Surfers Store, 1966. *Rod Sumpter Collection.* $30.

Dolphin wet suit ad, 1965. *Rod Sumpter Collection.* $25.

Otto and Jeanne's Surf Center, wallet card, 1963.
Rod Sumpter Collection. $25.

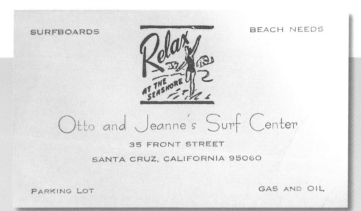

Hansen card, 1964. *Rod Sumpter Collection.* $25.

Windansea Surf Club card, 1964. *Rod Sumpter Collection.* $25.

Surf Shop envelope, 1962. *Rod Sumpter Collection.* $25.

Outrigger Canoe Club, letterhead, 1960.
Rod Sumpter Collection. $75.

International Surfing Championships, letterhead, 1964.
Rod Sumpter Collection. $25.

John Severson Productions, letterhead, 1960.
Rod Sumpter Collection. $30.

Chapter 8

Record Albums

"Surf Side," by The Denver Men, on RCA records, 1964-65. 45 rpm. Extended play from Australia. *Jamie & Maria Clark Collection.* $50-75.

"Surfing Seminar – World's Greatest Surfers Give Inside Tips On Surfing Technique," with Mike Doyle, Joey Cabell, Mickey Munoz, Joyce Hoffman, Del Cannon, and Chuck Linnen. LP 600-1/2, 1966-67. *Jamie & Maria Clark Collection.* $75-100.

"Surf War, The Battle Of The Surf Groups," by The Centurians, The Deltas, The Impaets, Bob Vaught and the Renegaids, and Dave Myers and the Surftones, 1963. On Shepherd records SLP-1300. Five leading surf groups from Southern California in a musical surf battle. *Jamie & Maria Clark Collection.* $75-150.

"Surfers Nightmare," by The Persuaders and Chuck (Tequila) Rio, on Saturn records SAT-500, 1963. *Jamie & Maria Clark Collection.* $75-300.

"Breakthrough," by Adrian and the Sunsets, on Sunset records SE 63-601, 1963. *Jamie & Maria Clark Collection.* $75-300.

"Waikiki Surf Battle," battle of eighteen bands, recorded live at the Waikiki Shell on September 14, 1963. *Jamie & Maria Clark Collection.* $125-400.

"Surfer's Slide," by Richie Allen and the Pacific Surfers, on Imperial records, LP 9243, 1963. *Jamie & Maria Clark Collection.* $50-150.

"Surfers' Holiday," by The Nep-Tunes, on Family records SFLP 552, 1963. *Jamie & Maria Clark Collection.* $75-250.

"Soul Surfin'," by The Rhythm Rockers on Challenge records, CH 617, 1963. *Jamie & Maria Clark Collection.* $50-200.

"The Soul Surfer," by Johnny Fortune on Park Ave. Records, P1301, 1963. *Jamie & Maria Clark Collection.* $75-300.

"The Rising Surf," by Richie Allen And The Pacific Surfers, on Imperial records, LP 9229, 1963. *Jamie & Maria Clark Collection.* $50-150.

"Surfin' Wild," by Jim Waller and The Deltas, on Arvee Records, A 432, 1963. *Jamie & Maria Clark Collection.* $50-200.

"Bustin' Surfboards," by The Tornadoes, on Josie Records, 4005, 1963. *Jamie & Maria Clark Collection.* $100-300.

"Surfin Around," by Billy Lazar and The Woody Wagoners, on Scarlett Records, SCM 100. 1963-64(?). $25-75.

"Surf Mania," by The Surf Teens on Sutton Records, SSU 339, 1963. Another classic beach scene cover shot. *Jamie & Maria Clark Collection.* $20-60.

"Shake! Shout! & Soul!" by Lil' Ray, The Original Surfaris, Dave Myers & The Surftones, The New-Dimensions, Steve Korey, 1964. *Jamie & Maria Clark Collection.* $75-250.

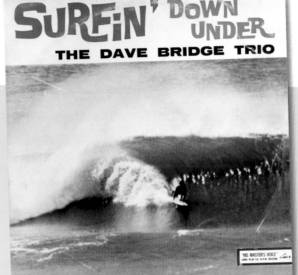

"Surfin' Down Under," by The Dave Bridge Trio, on RCA records, OCLP 7608, 1965. *Jamie & Maria Clark Collection.* $100-300.

"Let's Go Surfside," with The Denvermen, on RCA records, L101537, 1966. *Jamie & Maria Clark Collection.* $75-250.

"Only Startin'," by The Half Tribe, 1965. Includes surf theme track. *Jamie & Maria Clark Collection.* $400-900.

"Good Humor Presents Real Cool Hits," by The Avengers VI, on Mark 56 Records, no #, 1966. Includes surf theme track. *Jamie & Maria Clark Collection.* $125-400.

"Introducing The Aces Combo," by The Aces Combo, on Justice records JLP-134 A/B, 1965-66. Includes surf theme track. *Jamie & Maria Clark Collection.* $300-500.

"The Phantom Raiders...New Sound '67," by The Phantom Raiders, on Justice Records, JLP 151, 1967. Includes surf theme tracks. *Jamie & Maria Clark Collection.* $60.

Chapter 9
Trophies and Plaques

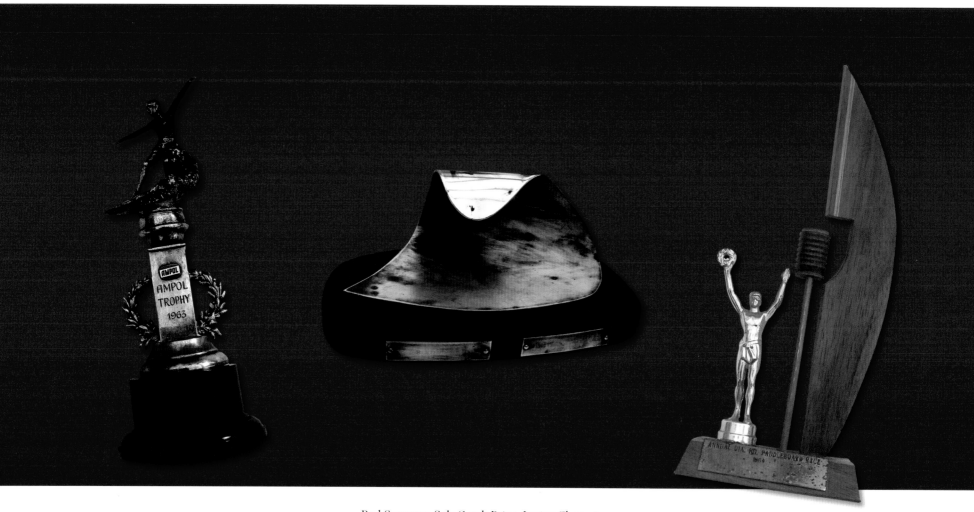

Rod Sumpter, Salt Creek Paipo Junior Champion, 1963. *Rod Sumpter Collection.* $300.

Rod Sumpter, 1st Australian Junior Championships, 1963. *Rod Sumpter Collection.* $3000.

Rod Sumpter, 3rd Diamond Head 6 mile paddle, 1964. *Rod Sumpter Collection.* $200.

Rod Sumpter, 5th World Championships,
1966. *Rod Sumpter Collection.* $4000.

Rod Sumpter, Three Time British Champion,
1965-67. *Rod Sumpter Collection.* $1100.

Rod Sumpter, Great Britain Open Champion,
1967. *Rod Sumpter Collection.* $700.

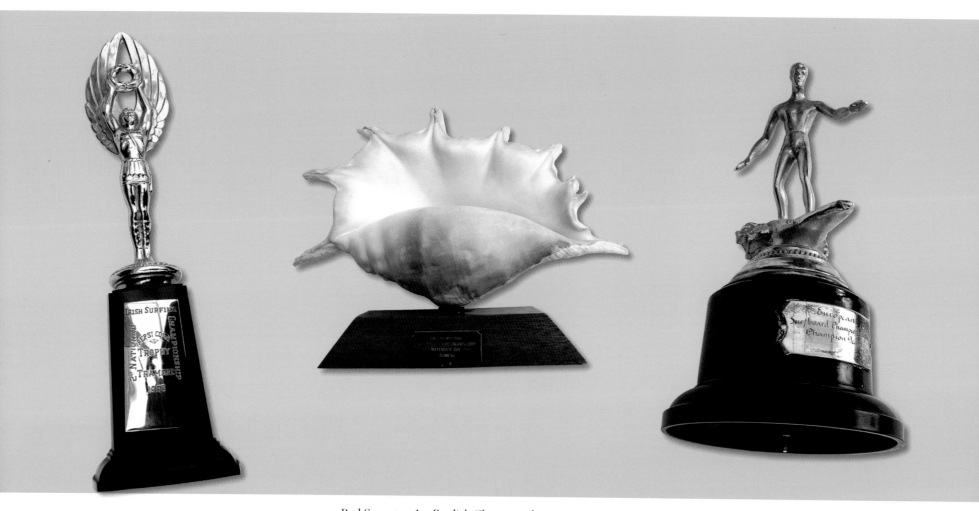

Rod Sumpter, 1st English Championships, 1969. *Rod Sumpter Collection.* $250.

Rod Sumpter, European Champion, 1969. *Rod Sumpter Collection.* $900.

Rod Sumpter, 1st Place, Irish International Championships, Tramore 1967 and 1968. $450.

Cornish Open Championship plaque,
1968. *Rod Sumpter Collection.* $50.

Rod Sumpter, 1st Group Two World Championships,
1966. *Rod Sumpter Collection.* $500.

G.B. National Surfboard Riding Championship plaque,
1967. *Rod Sumpter Collection.* $30.

Brochure for "Hawaiian Hollow Surfboard," invented by Tom Blake (surfboard expert of Waikiki Beach, Honolulu), c. 1930s. *Jamie & Maria Clark Collection.* $150-400.

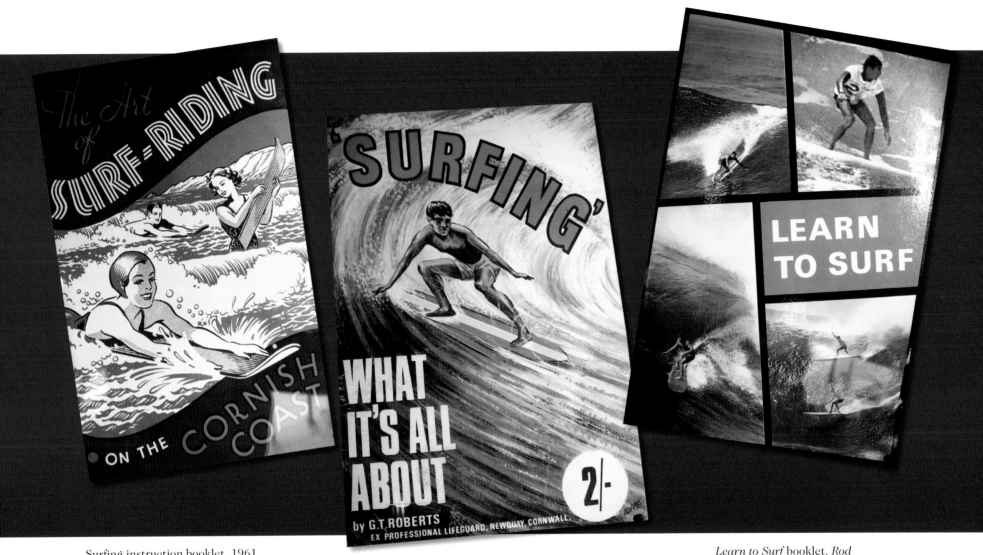

Surfing instruction booklet, 1961.
Rod Sumpter Collection. $75.

Surfing instruction booklet, 1967.
Rod Sumpter Collection. $30.

Learn to Surf booklet. *Rod
Sumpter Collection. $40.*

British Surfing Association
18 Bournemouth Road
Parkstone, Poole, Dorset

May 1978

Dear

Please find enclosed an invitation from the British Surfing Association to meet our Patron, H R H The Prince of Wales, on 8th June 1978. Prince Charles has expressed a wish to meet Champion and former Champion Surfers, representatives of the Executive Committee and others who have been helpful in developing surfing in Great Britain. As this will be held at Buckingham Palace, I feel a little guidance will be welcomed by most guests involved.

Whilst it is to be an informal party we would advise Men guests to wear lounge suits, sports jackets or international blazers. (Obviously, on this occasion, ties must be worn.) Ladies may wear either long or short dresses. I am afraid that cameras are not allowed inside the Palace and please be prepared to have handbags searched (especially the ladies).

Security at the Palace is obviously strict so please note that the invitation is only for the person, or persons, named on the invitation. Please bring them with you as they will be checked at the gate. Cars will be allowed inside the quadrangle for dropping off guests and parking will be provided inside the grounds. For this purpose, a special windscreen sticker will be issued after you have returned the tear-off slip at the foot of this letter. If you are travelling by train, then taxi, a sticker will be provided for you to give to the taxi driver to allow him to drop you off inside the palace quadrangle. Entrance on this occasion to Buckingham Palace will be through the right hand gate as you approach down The Mall. Police will be on that gate and will direct you through the centre arch in the Palace to the quadrangle.

I want you all to enjoy yourselves so do not worry about the formalities, they are quite simple. When Prince Charles speaks to you, it is quite in order to address him as 'Sir' although, if you wish when introduced for the first time, you may address him as 'Your Royal Highness'.

Please note the party is due to start at 6 pm but it will be in order for you to enter the Palace grounds after 5.30 pm and we would like everyone to be inside by 5.45 pm.

Finally, as this is basically a private party, we would ask you not to contact your local press or to give the reception too much publicity generally. We do not, of course, expect you to keep this invitation from your families and close friends, as I'm sure that is asking too much.

Please send in the acceptance slip as soon as possible informing us of the details as listed on the slip. We ask you to do this by return as final numbers need to be in the hands of the Equerry to the Prince of Wales at the soonest possible date to help him with the arrangements.

Yours sincerely,

Reginald J Prytherch
Chairman

Invitation from the British Surfing Association to meet with The Prince of Wales at Buckingham Palace, 1978. *John Baxendale Collection.* $50.

Letter accompanying invitation to Buckingham Palace, 1978. *John Baxendale Collection.* $30.

British team headed to Buckingham Palace party, 1978. *John Baxendale Collection.* $40.

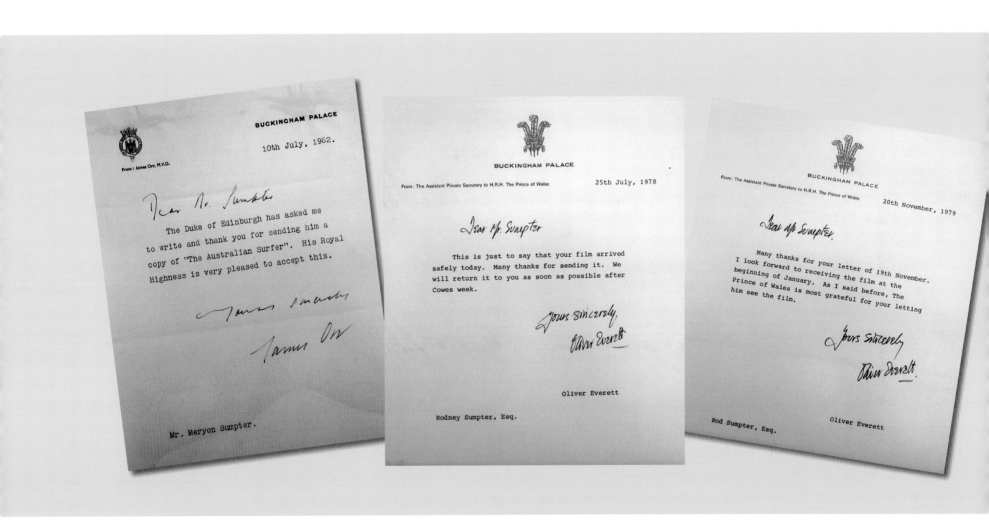

Royal letter, 1962. *Rod Sumpter Collection.* $900.

Royal letter, 1978. *Rod Sumpter Collection.* $100.

Royal letter, 1979. *Rod Sumpter Collection.* $150.

Letter from Irish surfer Kevin Cavey, 1968.
Rod Sumpter Collection. $40.

BRAY IRELAND SURF CLUB,
MOUNT HERBERT, BRAY.

Mr. Rod Sumpter,
c/o European Surfing Center,
Cornwall,
England.

BRITISH BOARD
OF FILM CENSORS
3, SOHO SQUARE LONDON W.1.

President
The Rt. Hon. The Lord Harlech K.C.M.G.

PRESIDENT *Harlech*

SECRETARY *Stephen Murphy*

FIVE SUMMER STORIES

THIS FILM HAS BEEN PASSED

A

NEWQUAY
On the Coast of Cornwall
TRAVEL BY TRAIN
BRITISH RAILWAYS

Five Summer Stories certificate, 1975. *Rod
Sumpter Collection.* $25.

Newquay poster, 1960. *Rod
Sumpter Collection.* $50.

Surfers Sandance poster, 1964.
Rod Sumpter Collection. $50.

Interstate Surf Meet poster, 1963.
Rod Sumpter Collection. $750.

Surfaris poster, 1972. *Rod Sumpter Collection.* $25.

Radio station poster, 1963. *Rod Sumpter Collection.* $50.

Postcard, "The Official Inauguration of the World Surfing Championship," 1965. *Rod Sumpter Collection.* $50.

Pro-Am poster, 1972. 34" x 22". *Jamie & Maria Clark Collection.* $400-800.

Postcard, "Surfboards by Phil," 1964.
Rod Sumpter Collection. $25.

Jersey poster, 1969. *Rod Sumpter Collection.*

1962 *Surfer* magazine calendar.
Rod Sumpter Collection. $50.

Huntington Surf Theatre card, 1970.
Rod Sumpter Collection. $25.

Huntington Surf Theatre schedule, 1971.
Rod Sumpter Collection. $30.

Bells Beach, first surfboard rally,
1961. *Rod Sumpter Collection.* $150.

Surf drawing, unknown artist, 1960.
Rod Sumpter Collection. $50.

(ABDULS) "RINCON SPECIAL"

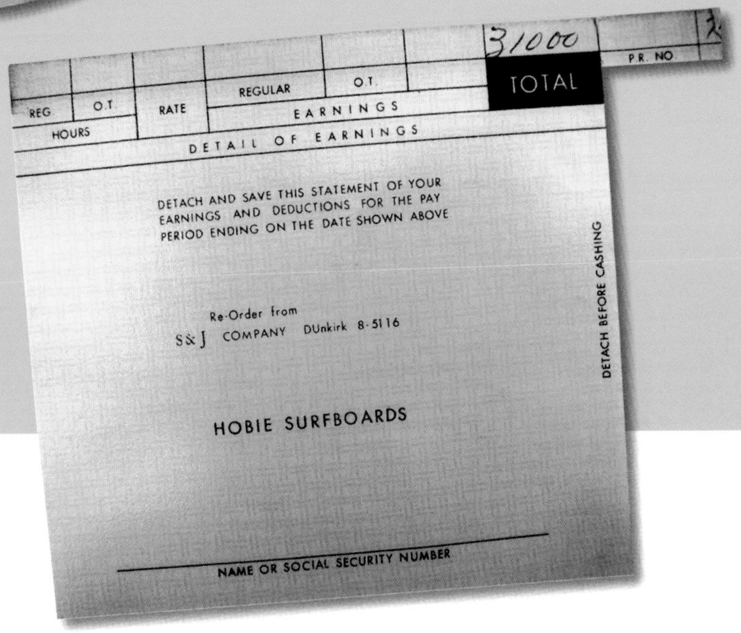

SURF LIFE SAVING ASSN G.B.

National
Surfboard Registration
No   468

REGISTRATION

31000

REG	O.T.	RATE	REGULAR	O.T.	TOTAL	P.R. NO.
HOURS			EARNINGS			
			DETAIL OF EARNINGS			

DETACH AND SAVE THIS STATEMENT OF YOUR
EARNINGS AND DEDUCTIONS FOR THE PAY
PERIOD ENDING ON THE DATE SHOWN ABOVE

Re-Order from
S & J COMPANY   DUnkirk 8-5116

HOBIE SURFBOARDS

DETACH BEFORE CASHING

NAME OR SOCIAL SECURITY NUMBER

Permit, Surf Life Saving Assn G.B., 1967.
Rod Sumpter Collection. $25.

Hobie Surfboards payslip, 1964.
Rod Sumpter Collection. $25.

Huntington patch from board shorts, 1963.
Rod Sumpter Collection. $30.

Council license decals, 1970-71.
Graham Looker Collection. $140.

Rod Sumpter competition board shorts, 1964-66.
Rod Sumpter Collection. $600.

Newquay patch from board shorts, 1965. *Rod Sumpter Collection.* $25.

Portugal patch from board shorts, 1965. *Rod Sumpter Collection.* $20.

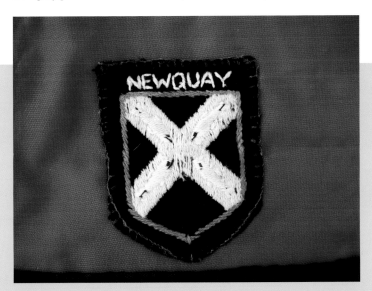

Avalon Point patch from board shorts, 1964.
Rod Sumpter Collection. $20.

"Hang Ten" patch from board shorts, 1964.
Rod Sumpter Collection. $45.

Cloth badge, British Surfing Association, 1978. *John Baxendale Collection.* $25.

Bilbo patch, 1966. *Rod Sumpter Collection.* $25.

Endless Summer patch. *Rod Sumpter Collection.* $25.

A first place ribbon won by the Outrigger Club in the "First Annual Citywide Surfboard Paddling Championships," held in Ala Wai Honolulu on December 1, 1929. On this day, Tom Blake set a new record and won the Surfboard Paddling Championship on his newly designed Hollow Surfboard. *Jamie & Maria Clark Collection.* $1000.

Rod Sumpter Bilbo, 9'8", 1965.
Rod Sumpter Collection. $1300.

Rod Sumpter design, Long Island, 1968.
Rod Sumpter Collection. $700.

Lamp from the surf spot Cape Three Points,
Ghana, 1967. *Rod Sumpter Collection.* $500.

Rod Sumpter shaped Bilbo, 9'7", 1965.
Simon Skelton Collection. $1100.

Model surfboards given out by the Waikiki Rotary Club. *Jamie & Maria Clark Collection.* $75-125.

Koa wood model surfboards sold as tourist souvenirs in the 1920s and '30s. *Jamie & Maria Clark Collection.* $125-200.